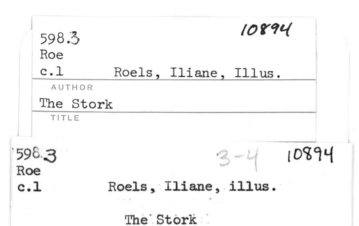

598.3
Roe
c.1   Roels, Iliane, Illus.   10894
     AUTHOR
The Stork
     TITLE

598.3   3-4   10894
Roe
c.1   Roels, Iliane, illus.

           The Stork

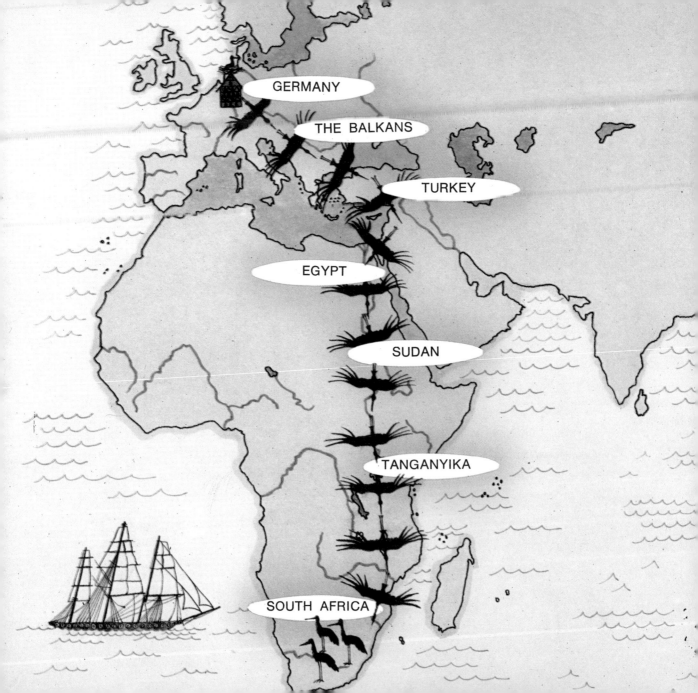

GERMANY

THE BALKANS

TURKEY

EGYPT

SUDAN

TANGANYIKA

SOUTH AFRICA

Animals at Home

The Stork

Idea and Illustrations by Iliane Roels

Translated by Marion Koenig

GROSSET & DUNLAP · NEW YORK

Published by Grosset & Dunlap, Inc. 1969

Published in Great Britain and English Translation
© 1969 by W. & R. Chambers Ltd, 11 Thistle Street, Edinburgh 2
© 1969 I.C.I. (International Copyright Institute)

Printed in Belgium 1969 by Van den Bossche S.A.

Library of Congress Catalog Card Number: 74-93444

High up on the roof of a German farmhouse there is a stork's nest. The farmer is very proud of it. Some years ago, he set an old cartwheel on the ridge of his roof. He hoped that a pair of storks would build their nest on it. But storks have become very scarce in Europe, and everywhere else too. For a long time the farmer waited in vain. Then, one day in spring, when all the birds came back from their winter journey to the south, two storks came with them. They looked for a good place to build a nest—a roof, or tower, or the reedy shore of a lake.

All of a sudden, they discovered the cartwheel. That was just what they had been looking for. Besides, there were marshy fields nearby, where they would find more than enough frogs. And since frogs are what storks like to eat most, they decided to build their nest here. Soon they had carried up twigs and feathers in their beaks—as well as thorny creepers, rags and grass. The female stork began to weave them all together. Suspicious, the two storks kept guard to see that no one stole their precious building materials. In eight days the nest was ready. It was big, and sturdy and round, and safe from wind and weather.

At the end of April, the female stork laid one white egg. After a few days she laid a second, then a third. They were almost as big as geese eggs, with shells that were a bit shiny. While the female sat on the eggs, the male stork looked after her. He brought her frogs, mice and snakes to eat and was very polite. Each time he returned to the nest, he raised his bill and made a loud clattering sound. Then the female stork would stand up and clatter her beak back at him.

The male stork often took his turn sitting on the eggs. But every evening, after a lot of pushing and fluffing out of feathers, they settled down on the eggs together. A month after the eggs had been laid, the baby storks hatched. Now three helpless balls of fluff lie in the nest. At first they are only covered in short, white fluff and their legs are pink instead of red.

Busily the father stork fastens new twigs to the nest so that the babies will not fall out. The three babies are always hungry. They are given worms, beetles and caterpillars to eat. From the first days of their lives they are not fed like other baby birds. The stork parents chew the food, then throw it into the nest. The babies have to pick it up and swallow it by themselves. After three weeks each of the babies already needs about one pound of meat a day. The parent storks also carry water to the nest in their crops. When the weather is very hot, they spray the babies and, sometimes, the big storks even spread their wings over the babies to protect them from the rain or the sun.

The young storks grow bigger and stronger. The nest becomes more and more cramped. Already they are clattering their little bills and learning how to speak like their parents. They clatter loudly, they clatter softly, sometimes they clatter slowly, sometimes fast. They clatter playfully, they clatter sadly. And how they clatter when they are hungry!

Then comes the day when life begins to get serious: they must start learning to fly. They stand on the edge of the nest excitedly flapping their wings. Their parents show them how it is done. But it is

not as easy as it looks. At first the little storks only get as far as
the ridge of the roof and the next time only as far as the barn. But
every day they get better. Then comes the great day when they
join their parents hunting for frogs in the marches.

This hunting territory belongs only to them. No heron or other stork is allowed to hunt there. The three walk along behind their parents. The female stork catches one frog after the other. In jerky movements she seizes her prey and, with a skilful flick of her head, lets it disappear into her beak. The young storks try to copy her. In the beginning the frogs are still too quick for the young storks and they escape. But, the youngest does manage to catch a toad. At once the mother tears it away from him.

Toads are not for storks! They dislike them more than any other animal. The stork will kill a toad but never eat it. Next, the parents rob birds' nests and gulp down any beetles, gnats and dragonflies that fly past. Whoever catches something must not bend down, otherwise it will slide out of his beak. Then the storks chase snakes in the shallow water. One of the young storks swallows an adder. It bites and wriggles in his throat. His neck hurts him for days afterwards even though he does not die of the poison. He will never swallow a poisonous snake again without killing it first.

Storks are dreadful thieves. They don't even spare moor hens and rabbits. Soon the young storks are as good at catching food as their parents. They lurk outside mouseholes. They grab moles. They chase grass hoppers. For the time being they still return home every night. Later on, they will lead their own lives.

Towards the end of July, the time for their great journey draws near. Before setting off, all the storks in the neighborhood gather in a certain meadow. Every day new ones arrive. At last they all set off. Loudly clattering, they circle over their home fields for a while. Then they turn and fly off into the distance.

Their destination is Africa. More and more of the big white wading birds join the flock. The young birds fly on ahead. None of the older birds shows them the way. In spite of that they never get lost. The flight is long and difficult and there are many dangers. Only the strong birds will last the whole journey. Those storks which live west of the River Weser choose a western route. They cross the Straits of Gibraltar and the Sahara Desert.

Then they fly high above the rain forests of the Congo to South Africa. But the storks which live east of the River Weser follow an eastern route, as do our three young storks. They and their parents travel across the Balkans and the Bosphorus to Asia Minor. Below them the domes of the mosques, the towers of the minarets and the Sea of Galilee gleam in the sunshine.

At last, far below, they can see a broad river—the Nile. Here, at the foot of the pyramids, where the storks meet other groups of travellers from Europe, they make a lengthy halt. For the young storks it is all new and strange, the animals, the plants, the people. They go hunting in the papyrus marshes and wade through the mud of the Nile, in order to recover from their long, exhausting flight. But they must always watch out for the crocodiles which lurk near the shore. Many an innocent stork has lost his life here. Then the journey goes on, across the plains and jungles to South Africa. Often the storks see peculiar dark clouds moving below them. These dark clouds are the swarms of locusts, flying down on fields to destroy the harvests. The storks follow the locusts. They dive at these pests and gobble up many of them. Afterwards they are so full that they can hardly move.

The life of the storks in Africa is quite different from that in Europe. They don't build nests, either on roofs or in trees. At night they sleep in little flocks on the banks of rivers and by day they hunt in the grassy plains. Soon the three young storks have made friends with a baboon. But in February, when the African autumn begins, the storks feel the urge to travel north again. Travelling by the same route as they came, they return to the place where they were born—preferably to their old nest. But year after year more of the waiting nests stay empty. The storks become scarcer, fewer and fewer return and nobody knows exactly why.

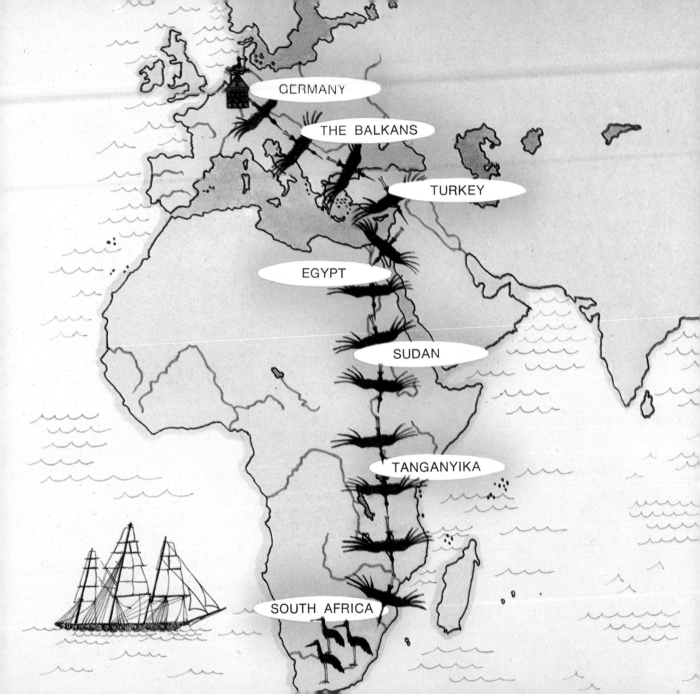

GERMANY

THE BALKANS

TURKEY

EGYPT

SUDAN

TANGANYIKA

SOUTH AFRICA

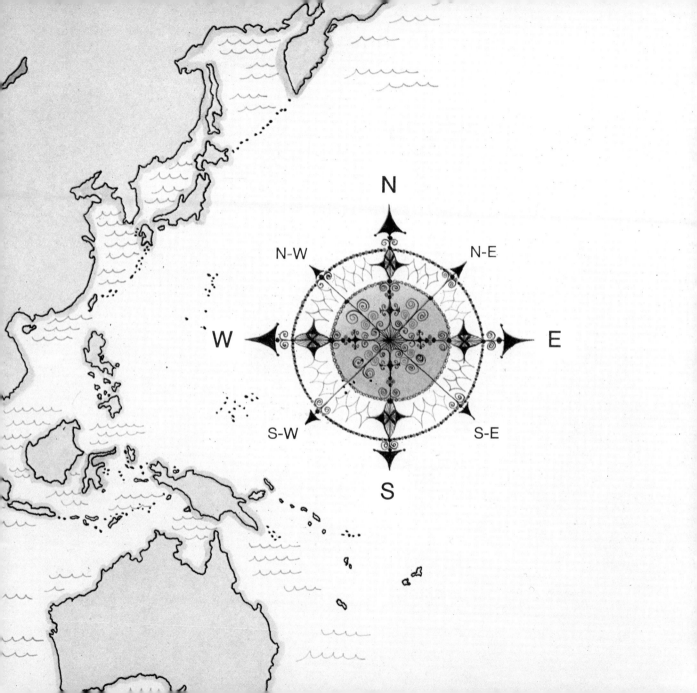